PRAY ALONG

A PREGNANT WOMAN'S PRAYER GUIDE

MARTINA SHARON K JOY

Copyright © Martina Sharon K Joy
All Rights Reserved.

This book has been published with all efforts taken to make the material error-free after the consent of the author. However, the author and the publisher do not assume and hereby disclaim any liability to any party for any loss, damage, or disruption caused by errors or omissions, whether such errors or omissions result from negligence, accident, or any other cause.

While every effort has been made to avoid any mistake or omission, this publication is being sold on the condition and understanding that neither the author nor the publishers or printers would be liable in any manner to any person by reason of any mistake or omission in this publication or for any action taken or omitted to be taken or advice rendered or accepted on the basis of this work. For any defect in printing or binding the publishers will be liable only to replace the defective copy by another copy of this work then available.

To every mom-to-be...

Contents

Acknowledgements

I would like to thank the God Almighty for inspiring me
with the thought of creating a Rosary book dedicated to all
the Moms- to- be.
And love to my husband, Jayanth, who has always been
a great source of motivation and support through all the
ups and downs in life.

I

The Couple's Prayer

Blessed are you Lord our God, King of the Universe, for you have brought us both together to carry out your plan for us. Thank you for all the blessings that you have given us. Help us to see the good in each other and deepen our relation with humility and respect. And above all help us to put on love, which binds everything in perfect harmony. Amen!

II
Prayer to St. Gerard

(Patron Saint of all expectant mothers)
To be recited daily
O great Saint Gerard, beloved servant of Jesus Christ, perfect imitator of your meek and humble Savior, and devoted child of Mother of God, enkindle within my heart one spark of that heavenly fire of charity which glowed in your heart and made you an angel of love. O glorious Saint Gerard, because when falsely accused of crime, you did bear, like your Divine Master, without murmur or complaint, the calumnies of wicked men, you have been raised up by God as the patron and protector of expectant mothers. Preserve me from danger and from the excessive pains accompanying childbirth, and shield the child which I now carry, that it may see the light of day and receive the purifying and life-giving waters of baptism through Jesus Christ our Lord.
Amen!

III

The Holy Rosary

IN THE NAME of the Father, and of the Son, and of the Holy Spirit. Amen.

I BELIEVE IN GOD, the Father almighty, Creator of Heaven and earth. I believe in Jesus Christ, His only Son, our Lord, He was conceived by the power of the Holy Spirit, and born of the Virgin Mary, suffered under Pontius Pilate; was crucified, died, and was buried. He descended unto the Dead. On the third day, he rose again from the dead. He ascended into Heaven, and is seated at the right hand of the Father. He will come again to judge the living and the dead. I believe in the Holy Spirit, the holy Catholic Church, the communion of saints, the forgiveness of sins, the resurrection of the body, and the life everlasting. Amen

OUR FATHER, Who art in Heaven, hallowed be Thy Name. Thy kingdom come, Thy will be done on earth as it is in Heaven. Give us this day our daily bread, and forgive us our trespasses, as we forgive those who trespass against us. And lead us not into temptation, but deliver us from evil. Amen.

HAIL MARY, full of grace, the Lord is with thee. Blessed art thou among women, and blessed is the fruit of thy womb, Jesus. Holy Mary, Mother of God, pray for us sinners, now and at the hour of our death. Amen.

GLORY BE to the Father, and to the Son, and to the Holy Spirit. As it was in the beginning is now, and ever shall be, world without end. Amen.

O MY JESUS, forgive us our sins, save us from the fires of Hell; lead all souls to Heaven, especially those in most need of Thy mercy. Amen.

HAIL HOLY QUEEN, mother of mercy; our life, our sweetness, and our hope. To thee do we cry, poor banished children of Eve. To thee do we send up our sighs, mourning and weeping in this vale of tears. Turn, then, most gracious advocate, thine eyes of mercy toward us. And after this, our exile, show unto us the blessed fruit of thy womb, Jesus. O clement, O loving, O sweet Virgin Mary. Pray for us, O holy Mother of God, that we may be made worthy of the promises of Christ. Amen.

LET US PRAY: O God, whose only-begotten Son by His life, death and resurrection, has purchased for us the rewards of eternal life; grant, we beseech Thee, that by meditating upon these mysteries of the Most Holy Rosary of the Blessed Virgin Mary, we may imitate what they contain and obtain what they promise, through the same Christ our Lord. Amen.

ෆ

We then start with the part of the rosary, anouncing the decades of the rosary based on the Mystery for each day. Please find below the different mysteries recited on different days and then go ahead with the Rosary. Note that each set of Mystery has 5 sub- mysteries. After each sub mystery the intention is stated and the 10 Hail Mary's follow.

Joyful Mysteries (On Mondays / and Saturdays and Sundays of Advent and Christmas)

- The Annunciation.
- The Visitation.
- The Nativity.
- The Presentation of Jesus at the Temple.
- The Finding of Jesus in the Temple.

Luminous Mysteries (On Thursdays)

- The Baptism of Jesus in the Jordan.
- The Wedding at Cana.
- Jesus' Proclamation of the Kingdom of God.
- The Transfiguration.
- The Institution of the Eucharist.

Sorrowful Mysteries (On Tuesdays, Fridays/ and Saturdays of Lent)

- The Agony in the Garden.
- The Scourging at the Pillar.
- The Crowning with Thorns.
- The Carrying of the Cross.
- The Crucifixion and Death of our Lord.

Glorious Mysteries (On Wednesdays and Sundays of Easter and Ordinary time)

- The Resurrection.
- The Ascension.

- The Descent of the Holy Spirit.
- The Assumption of Mary.
- The Coronation of the Virgin.

ജ

INTRODUCTION
1. IN THE NAME...
2. I BELIEVE IN GOD...
3. OUR FATHER...
(3 HAIL MARY'S)
4. GLORY BE...
5. O MY JESUS...

ജ

THE FIRST DECADE (In this decade we pray for all the childless couples. For those who are not able to face the society with their questions. For those who have waited a long time and feel disappointed that you have not heard their voice. We pray for all women dealing with Infertility issues and for those who are being rejected by their own spouse/ family members for this reason. For in Isaiah 54:1 the Lord says, 'Sing O barren one, who did not bear; break forth into singing and cry aloud, you who have not been in labour! For the children of the desolate one will be more than the children of her who is married.'. Help them to take the example of Sarah- who at her oldage bore a son, while they called her 'barren'. *For this we pray.....*)
1. OUR FATHER...
2. (10 HAIL MARY' S)
3. GLORY BE...
4. O MY JESUS...

ജ

THE SECOND DECADE (In this decade we pray for all the new moms to be. Especially for the ones who are not able to accept this gift from God or have received this great blessing without planning and that everything is perfect in God's plan. We pray that they realize that they have been called to be co creators with God. Help them understand that the fruit of the womb is a reward. We pray that they are able to give thanks along with their spouses for this great blessing that they have received. *For this we pray.....*)
1. OUR FATHER...
    2. (10 HAIL MARY' S)
    3. GLORY BE...
    4. O MY JESUS...

૪૭

THE THIRD DECADE (In this decade we pray for all the women who have undergone miscarriages and losses during pregnancy. We pray that the mighty Lord will cast away all the fears and instill in them the spirit of Hope and courage. We pray that they recover soon from the struggles and pains that they have undergone and also pray that they look forward to leading their lives in the way God has planned for them. Help them realise that the Lord is close to the broken hearted, he rescues those whose spirits are crushed. Job 1:21b also states the Lord gave and the Lord has taken away, may the name of the Lord be praised. *For this we pray......*)
    1. OUR FATHER...
    2. (10 HAIL MARY' S)
    3. GLORY BE...
    4. O MY JESUS...

૪૭

THE FOURTH DECADE (In this decade we pray for all the women who resort to abortion and child pregnancy. Help them understand that the gift of a child is and that abortions are nothing different from murder. Whatever be the reason, our Lord hates people who shed inocent blood. We pray that they understand this and ask God for his forgiveness. And for those who feel guilty for their act, we pray that the most merciful God shows his mercy and grants them forgiveness. We pray for all the couples contemplating to abort, that they may have a change in mind. Help them understand that career, fame, Physical body stature are all secondary. *For this we pray.....*)

1. OUR FATHER...
2. (10 HAIL MARY' S)
3. GLORY BE...
4. O MY JESUS...

THE FIFTH DECADE (In this decade we pray for all the unborn babies. For the Lord says, in Jeremiah 1:5,' Before I formed you in the womb, I knew you. Before you were born, I sanctified you. I have appointed you a prophet to the nations.' We pray that we are able to bring forth this precious little one, into the light of this world and then Baptize and raise him/her up in the true christian faith. *For this we pray.....*)

1. OUR FATHER...
2. (10 HAIL MARY' S)
3. GLORY BE...
4. O MY JESUS...

CONCLUSION

IV
Prayer through the pregnancy

God, you see the baby in my womb. You know her every detail. No matter how he/she is formed, he/she is beloved by you. Grant me the peace all through my pregnancy, and help me surrender every fear unto you. Lord Jesus I thank you for the protection over my life and my baby's life. For as long as this pregnancy lasts, I pray that you will be doing the mighty and marvelous work that only you can do, creating life and bringing beauty into the world. Thank you for chosing me to be a part of this miracle.

Amen!

V
Prayer for a safe delivery

Dear Lord, I Thank you for the miracle you are creating in me. I thank you for bringing me safely to the end my pragnancy journey. Anoint my body that I may have a safe delivery. I pray that you send your angels to keep guard of me as my labour begins. Hold me through each wave of childbirth. I pray for all the proffessionals who have been a part of this amazing journey and in special pray for those who are going to handlle this delivery. You grew us both in your image and I trust in your plan.

May my baby be born in your perfect image. I pray that your mighty hand will be with him/ her all through his/ her life and that he/ she grows without any health problems.

In Jesus name I pray, Amen!

WISHING YOU A SAFE DELIVERY!

"Dont worry about the things you can cannot control, just focus on what you can do."

I pray that you have a safe delivery and spread the word about the book to those who are in need....
Do pray for me!

www.ingramcontent.com/pod-product-compliance
Lightning Source LLC
Chambersburg PA
CBHW071315130726
47997CB00007B/2571